W9-BXX-531

Kindness and Generosity:
It Starts with Me!

by Jodie Shepherd

Content Consultant
Samantha Gambino, Psy.D.
Licensed Psychologist, New York, New York

Reading Consultant
Jeanne M. Clidas, Ph.D.
Reading Specialist

Children's Press®
An Imprint of Scholastic Inc.

Library of Congress Cataloging-in-Publication Data
Shepherd, Jodie, author.
  Kindness & generosity : it starts with me / by Jodie Shepherd.
    pages cm. -- (Rookie talk about it)
  Summary: "Teaches the reader about kindness and generosity."-- Provided by publisher.
  ISBN 978-0-531-21516-6 (library binding) -- ISBN 978-0-531-21384-1 (pbk.) 1. Kindness--Juvenile literature.
2. Generosity--Juvenile literature. 3. Conduct of life--Juvenile literature. I. Title. II. Title: Kindness and
generosity.

  BJ1533.K5S54 2016
  177--dc23   2015018078

No part of this publication may be reproduced in whole or in part, or stored in a retrieval system, or
transmitted in any form or by any means, electronic, mechanical, photocopying, recording, or otherwise,
without written permission of the publisher. For information regarding permission, write to Scholastic Inc.,
Attention: Permissions Department, 557 Broadway, New York, NY 10012.

Produced by Spooky Cheetah Press
Design by Keith Plechaty

© 2016 by Scholastic Inc.

All rights reserved. Published in 2016 by Children's Press, an imprint of Scholastic Inc.

Printed in China 62

SCHOLASTIC, CHILDREN'S PRESS, ROOKIE TALK ABOUT IT™, and associated logos are trademarks and/or
registered trademarks of Scholastic Inc.

1 2 3 4 5 6 7 8 9 10 R 25 24 23 22 21 20 19 18 17 16

Photographs ©: cover: Mike Kemp/Media Bakery; 3 top left: MaMi/Shutterstock, Inc.; 3 top right: Media
Bakery; 3 bottom: Jamie Grill/JGI/Media Bakery; 4: Media Bakery; 7: Ron Chapple/Media Bakery; 8:
Jamie Grill/JGI/Media Bakery; 11: jf/Media Bakery; 12: Graham French/Masterfile; 15: RuslanDashinsky/
iStockphoto; 16: Steve Debenport/iStockphoto; 19: Terrie L. Zeller/Shutterstock, Inc.; 20: Keith Heneghan/
Alamy Images; 23: Media Bakery; 24: Aldo Murillo/iStockphoto; 26: Vivien Killilea/Getty Images; 27:
fotohunter/Shutterstock, Inc.; 28: Media Bakery; 29: vgajic/iStockphoto; 30: PaulMaguire/iStockphoto; 31 top:
Mike Kemp/Media Bakery; 31 center top: vgajic/iStockphoto; 31 center bottom: sevenke/Shutterstock, Inc.;
31 bottom: jf/Media Bakery.

Table of Contents

What Are Kindness and Generosity?

You open up your backpack. You realize you forgot to bring a snack to school! You do not say anything. But your friend notices you are not eating. She hands you one of her cookies. She is being both kind *and* generous.

Kindness means you think about other people's feelings, not just your own. A kind person helps others. It feels good to help someone else!

Generosity and kindness are a lot alike. A generous person is happy to share what she has.

You do not need to buy things for people to be generous. You can give a gift from the heart. You can make a card for a friend who is sick. You can give your brother a hug if he falls.

You can also give your time. Generous people **volunteer** to help others. You could volunteer for a big job, like helping to pick up garbage at a beach. Or you could volunteer for a small job, like reading a book to your little brother or sister.

"She has a heart of gold." Have you ever heard someone say that? It does not mean the person's heart is really made of gold. It is another way of saying that she is kind and generous. Maybe *you* have a heart of gold.

Read about some other kind kids. Think about what you would do if you were in their place.

Bighearted Heroes

Everyone was playing soccer at recess, and Ethan slipped and fell. He cut his knee. He is really upset. Josh stops playing to see if Ethan is okay. He puts his arm around his friend to try to make him feel better. Then he offers to walk Ethan to the nurse's office.

Noah's school is having a winter coat drive. The coats will go to people who really need them to keep warm. Noah has a coat that does not fit anymore. He really likes it, but he knows he will not wear it. Noah **donates** his coat to the drive. Helping others feels great!

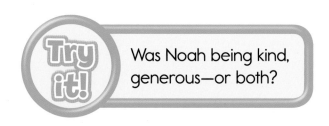

Try it!

Was Noah being kind, generous—or both?

It is Mia's birthday party. Her aunt says she is really excited for Mia to open her gift. Mia cannot wait to see what it is!

But when Mia opens the gift, she is **disappointed**. It is a book that she already has. She does not tell her aunt, though. She says, "Thank you so much!" And she gives her aunt a big hug.

Henry's neighbor broke her leg, and it is hard for her to walk her dog. Henry and his mom offer to help out. Henry walks his neighbor's dog every day before school. His neighbor is really **grateful**.

Lily and Aiden feel bad. Their friend Emma has been home sick all week. Now she is going to miss the 100th Day of School party. Lily, Aiden, and all their friends make a poster: "100 Things We Love About Emma." Lily brings it to her after school—along with some treats from the party.

Try it! How do you think Emma felt when her friend visited her after school?

What ways can you think of to be kind and generous? Whether they are big or small, they will help make the world a better and kinder place. They will make *you* feel good, too.

Lulu Cerone

Like most teenagers, Lulu Cerone likes parties. But Lulu makes her parties count!

When she was 10 years old, Lulu learned that each one-dollar cup of lemonade she sold could mean a whole year of clean water for someone in Africa. She held a lemonade sale with her classmates that raised more than $4,000 for the cause.

But Lulu did not stop there. She started an organization called LemonAID Warriors. It helps kids turn things they are already doing into chances to give. For example, a sleepover party can become a chance to collect blankets for homeless people. Lulu has given away thousands of dollars and inspired many people to help others. She even won a Nickelodeon HALO award for her work.

Practice being generous by making a Giving Jar:

You will need: a clean, empty jar; a label; colored markers; stickers; and paint

1. Write Giving on the label and stick it to the front of the jar.

2. Use the paint and stickers to decorate the jar.

3. Put part of your weekly allowance, or money you receive on special occasions, into the jar. Then, when the jar is full, donate the money to an organization of your choice.

Read the story below and imagine what you might do in this situation.

There was a big storm in your town, and some houses were flooded. A girl at school lost a lot of her clothes, toys, and books. Her parents bought her new clothes. But she is still sad about what she has lost.

Need help getting started?

- Do you have any books, toys, or stuffed animals that you can give to your friend?

- Is there something you might do or say to cheer her up?

29

How Generous Are You?

1. You are growing fast! Your clothes are still in good shape, but they do not fit anymore. What do you do?

   A. Throw them away and then look forward to buying new clothes.

   B. Donate some to a homeless shelter.

2. You just helped your mom bake a huge batch of your favorite cookies. What do you do?

   A. Say, "Oh, goody! Lots for me!"

   B. Put some aside to share with your friend at lunch tomorrow.

3. It is a warm, sunny day. Your brother is sick and has to stay inside. What do you do?

   A. Cheerfully wave good-bye and skip off to the swing set.

   B. Spend a little time first keeping your brother company, then go out and play.

If you answered mostly with Bs, you have a generous heart.

Glossary

disappointed (diss-uh-POIN-ted): feeling let down

donates (DOH-nayts): gives something to someone who needs it

grateful (GRAYT-fuhl): thankful for things

volunteer (vah-luhn-TEER): help out without being paid

Index

Facts for Now

Visit this Scholastic Web site for more information on kindness and generosity:
www.factsfornow.scholastic.com
Enter the keywords **Kindness and Generosity**

About the Author

Jodie Shepherd, who also writes under the name Leslie Kimmelman, is an award-winning author of dozens of books for children, both fiction and nonfiction. She is a children's book editor, too.